TINY HOUSE BUILDING

A practical guide for conversion from garage to tiny house

Bob and Katy Hollway

Tiny House Building
Copyright © 2015 Bob and Katy Hollway

SozoPrint
SozoPrint.com

ISBN 978-0-9929404-2-3

Contact or follow the author

www.KatyHollway.com
www.facebook.com/KatyHollwayAuthor
www.twitter.com/KatyHollway
www.pinterest.com/katyhollway/

CONTENTS

INTRODUCTION

I may be an author of fiction... but I am also a trained interior architect and married to a builder. Some might say is a great match since I can design and he can build, but inevitably it leads to slightly larger building projects than a set of shelves. We have been tackling a new building project in this last season.

This book has the words and pictures added by myself, but could not have been written without my husband. So that means that the authorship is definitely shared.

The recent enthusiasm for Tiny Houses is fuelled by such ideas as a simpler way of living, a lower or no mortgage, de-cluttering and a smaller impact on the environment. In America many have built their own Tiny Houses on trailers and can be transported on wheels. There are houses that have as little as 7.4m^2 floor space.

In England there aren't as many Tiny Houses on wheels, but there is a lack of affordable housing.

My husband and I have three children and live in Brighton, a seaside town on the south coast of the UK. Housing prices here tend to be above average since we are a commutable distance from London. I recently heard that the average person buying a house (still a preferred way of living in the UK) is in their mid-thirties. Up until they purchase their first home they are renting or choosing to stay with their parents for longer to save for that all important deposit.

We are blessed to live in a wonderful house on an unusual plot. But it has taken several moves to get to this house. I have lived through many renovations and extensions, even cooking in a kitchen made of pallets for a short while!

On our plot stood a garage, packed with our stuff but was serving as little else. It was old, tired and needed repair.

Our building project was sparked by a friend needing a place to live. She would have loved to be in her own place as she had been sharing with friends for several years, but there was just no way of doing that.

The garage could provide a solution for our friend and also add value to the property. So we talked and speculated about building a Tiny House. In the UK we would call such a Tiny House a "Granny Annex" or just simply a conversion.

In the following pages I hope to take you on that journey. My hope is that you will find information, inspiration and indication that you could possibly do the same.

Katy ;)

PLANNING

Vision

You have this book in your hand, so I am assuming that you have vision or at least a hope that there is a way of creating a tiny house.

We had a detached garage that was asking to be converted, but maybe you have a corner of land or the end of your garden. There are many companies that create garden rooms around the country. Some may look like sheds but there are some very stylish timber buildings too.

I don't have plans for timber garden buildings but hopefully this book will contain some useful information for you.

In Brighton, the council has recently used converted shipping containers as living spaces. I have seen plenty of images on the internet using this idea. Some of the designs are truly spectacular.

If you are heading down either of these routes, there are plenty of things over the next few pages that you will have to consider too.

This was our conversion subject.

It was a single garage with a small workshop at the end. The walls were sound with no cracks and the foundations were strong.

The thing with vision on a project like this, is that you have to imagine that the land, space or building could be something else.

Planning Permission

I looked at the local council website and tried to decipher the jargon (yes, even as a trained interior architect albeit one out of practice, found the wording and restrictions confusing), I had a rough idea of what I was allowed to do. I made notes and then booked an appointment with the planning department for an informal consultation to check that I had actually understood the information. This was a really helpful thing to do as the planning officer was able to direct me in how to go about submitting plans that were less likely to be rejected. He also pointed out some of the things that I missed in terms of roof heights and boundaries ... all important stuff. It was good idea to take photos, rough plans and various ideas with me into that appointment as the officer was able to dismiss anything that was an obvious no with regards to planning.

Things to look out for with regards to planning or building regulations:

Building near to boundaries – height restrictions under building regulations (walls and roof) In our case, if the building was closer than 1.5m to the boundary, the roof height had to be below 3.5m and the wall height below 2.5m. If you want to build outside the restrictions, you will need to obtain planning permission.

Windows – be careful about overlooking others. Your neighbours will be given opportunity to object to planning permission so retain privacy.

Use – are you aiming for a completely independent property or shared (I found that if the Tiny House had shared access, garden, services etc. that planning was not necessarily needed if I didn't raise the roof height.)

Listed building or Conservation area – this can include trees and permission may be needed to remove them.

Please note, there are rules about building a habitable dwelling that need to be adhered to, but likewise there are also ways of building a space that a person can sleep in but not "live in independently" because it has shared facilities with the main dwelling.

Overall, I would recommend making an appointment with the council planning officer. Take with you:

Rough plans with measurements

An ordinance survey map of where you live or a print out of google maps showing your property and others around it.

Photos of the site.

A notebook.

An open mind – the planning officer may be able to give you a better solution.

Structural

With the garage conversion we wanted to give a feeling of space, even though the actual space was small. We needed to increase the height of the roof to provide a "room" for sleeping in and add a new window.

These things would affect the structure of the building and the loads to the walls and ground.

In order for building regulations to be passed, structural calculations need to be done. Planning permission can be given without these calculations, but as building regulations will also have to be adhered to after you have permission, structural calculations cannot be avoided.

Unless you are a structural engineer, this is a skill that is best left to them. You do not want the roof falling in or a floor to collapse.

A structural engineer will work from drawings if they are accurate or can do a site visit.

In our case, the structural engineer (in this case a man) came for a visit because we wanted him to check foundations (see page 21) and to talk through with him the methods that we wanted to apply to the garage. If we had not shown him the space and told him what we were hoping to achieve he may have suggested a slightly different roof beam/structure or raised floor to what we wanted. It was important at this stage, before anything was built, that we knew what we could do and how to do it.

It is worth investing a little time and money in this as all you do will have to be based on these calculations.

Here is an example of a page from structural calculations.

You may get a computer drawn image or hand drawn.

The calculations should tell you what size beams, lintels and supports are needed, what they are made of and how they should be fitted.

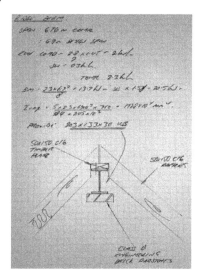

Drawing Plans

Before anything is drawn, take a moment to think about the services to your Tiny House. Questions like, "How is water going to get into the building?" "How is waste water going to get out?" "How do I heat the space and water?" "Where is the electricity supply coming from?"

We found out that a second gas meter would need to be fitted costing too much money so we opted for electric heating. This then affected how the electricity would then enter the building. It is best to have a clear idea of these unexciting but vital parts of the design. (See page 20)

Using the advice from the appointment with the planning officer, simple plans can be drawn. This is my skill and I was happy to get to work with it. It needn't be too difficult to do yourself especially if the council are not asking for planning permission and building regulations are just required.

Using squared paper, a scale drawing of the space can be produced.

You will need to accurately measure the structure that you already have or survey the site where the building will be going. Squared paper is useful for creating a right angled building, but you can use plain paper too. There are even some websites where a basic drawing can be made of the space including doors and windows.

For both planning permission and building regulations you will need:

Existing plans and elevations (1:100)

Proposed site plans and elevations (1:100)

Proposed floor plan with section (1:50)

Site plan (1:1250, 1:500) showing boundary of property.

These will have to be to scale and include a scale on the drawing (councils will place your drawings online so a drawn scale is needed for the public to access).

A good way of seeing what the council is after in terms of drawings is to check out their planning proposals that are underway. You should be able to access the drawings of new buildings being planned in your area by searching the council website.

On the next few pages you will be able to see the plans, elevations and sections that were submitted for the garage to Tiny House conversion

Drawings do not need to be submitted on huge A0 paper. A series of smaller pieces of paper, even A4, can be used. All my drawings were on A4 but arranged so that they made sense to the person viewing them.

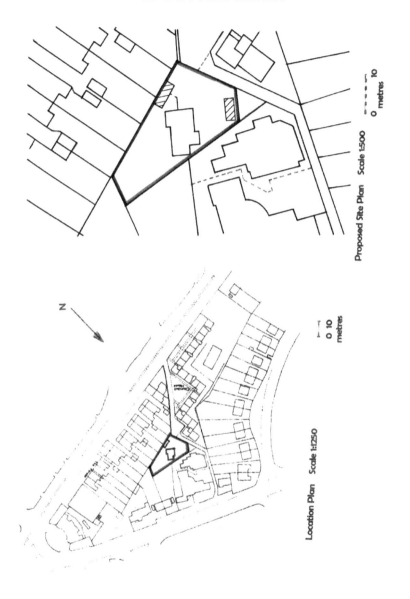

Keep the block plans together and try to orientate them in the same direction. Mark on the drawing the boundaries of your property (often this is asked to be marked in red).

Don't forget to include the address of the property and any reference numbers that are needed on the drawings (not shown here).

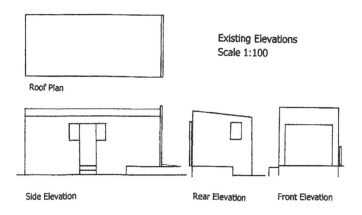

Existing Elevations
Scale 1:100

Roof Plan

Side Elevation

Rear Elevation

Front Elevation

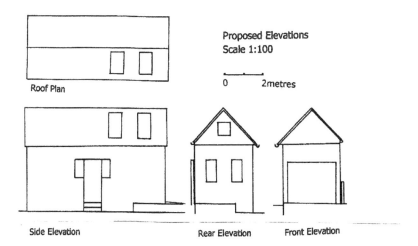

Proposed Elevations
Scale 1:100

0   2metres

Roof Plan

Side Elevation

Rear Elevation

Front Elevation

Existing and proposed put together can help others see what is being changed without too much confusion. The drawings were submitted to scale but there is also a scale bar (0-2m) to measure from.

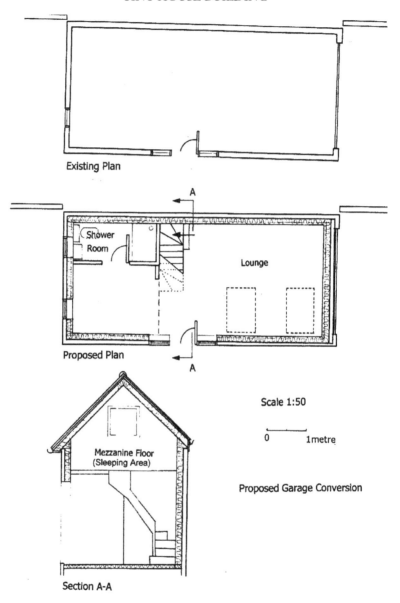

Existing Plan

Shower Room

Lounge

Proposed Plan

Scale 1:50

0   1metre

Proposed Garage Conversion

Mezzanine Floor
(Sleeping Area)

Section A-A

The plans at this scale should show more detail. You will need to add where partition walls are, staircases, doors, windows, insulation and wall thickness. It is also good to label the spaces that you are creating. However, you will notice that I did not label the kitchen area.

Building Regulations

Building regulations *seem to be* constantly changing. If you looked at the regulations that properties had to fall into just ten years ago, you would find that they have changed from today. But surprisingly, things haven't changed too much in the past couple of years. Councils seem to be content with the way buildings are converted and the rules they have had in place.

For building regulations you will need a whole load of technical jargon about insulation, access, ventilation, u-values ... With a bit of time on the internet, these things can be accessed but prepare yourself to be confused.

Below you will find the regulation jargon that was needed to be submitted alongside our drawings after planning permission was granted and the building regulation was applied for. These were correct for the south of England in 2014.

At this point it is worth remembering that both planning permission and building regulations have to be paid for separately. The amount of space and the work that you are undertaking will also vary the fee that is asked for. This can be confusing, so a quick call to the council office will save time later. You may have had planning permission granted, but until building regulations have been passed, your building is not legal. The council building inspectors will also visit on site at different points in the build to assure that the regulations are being adhered to. It is a good idea to read through the regulations and understand what you have said you will do.

This list is not to be applied to any building work that you are doing, and there may even be extra stipulations or less requirements that your council wants you to fulfil. You should be able to find the regulations online, although I spent several days looking for the information I needed. Hopefully the list that follows will get you started.

Specifications

The building regulations list should look something like this:

Planning Application Number - *Your application number*
Address of the property where work will take place

Conversion of *Existing Garage to Annex*

Foundations
Expose existing concrete footings prior to commencement of work.

DPC
Existing floor and 1m high on walls to be painted with damp proof paint.

Pitched Roof
Using 50 x 150mm pre-treated timbers at 400mm centres, with Tyvek breathable felt, 19 x 38mm pressure treated softwood battens. Concrete tiles fitted to manufacturers guidelines.
Velux roof window to be double trimmed.
Wall plate to be strapped with galvanised metal straps at 900mm centres.
100mm PIR thermal insulation boards to be cut between timbers. 15mm PIR thermal insulation boards to be overlaid with 12.5mm plasterboard and skim coat on top.

External Gable ends
Constructed from concrete blocks with Tyvek breathable felt, 19 x 38mm pressure treated softwood battens. Concrete tiles fitted to manufacturers guidelines.

Steel Beam
Beam to be fitted as per structural engineers drawings. Beam to be painted with half hour fire resistant paint and encased in 12.5mm Gyproc Fireline board.
Timber plate strapped to steel beam at 900mm centres.

Lintels
All lintels on lower level to be single skin galvanised steel.
Higher level lintel to be 100 x 140mm pcc as per structural drawings.

Windows/Door
Windows and doors to be uPVC double glazed with low-E soft coat.

All windows to be fitted with trickle vents.
Door, window next to door and upper window to be fitted with toughened safety glass. Upper window to have fire escape hinge and lead tray dressed round tile hanging.

Electrics
All electrical work required to meet the requirements of Part P (electrical safety)to be designed, installed, inspected and tested by a competent person registered under a competent person self certification scheme such as BRE certification Ltd, BSI, NICEIC Certification Services or Zurich Ltd. An appropriate BS7671 Electrical Installation Certificate is to be issued for the work by a person competent to do so. A copy of a certificate will be given to the Council.

Heating
All heating and hot water services from independent source and provide new TVRs to radiators. Heating system to be designed, installed, tested and fully certified by a GAS SAFE registered specialist. All work to be in accordance with the Local Water Authorities bye laws, Gas safety requirements and IEEE regulations.

Smoke/Fire Alarm
Provide proprietary mains powered smoke and heat detectors with battery back up to BS 5446 Part 1:2000 and Part 3:2004at least a Grade D category LD3 standard.

Staircase/Balustrade
Dimensions to be checked and measured on site prior to fabrication of stairs. Timber stairs to comply with BS585 and with Part K of the Building Regulations.
Balustrade to be designed with no opening large enough to allow a sphere of 100mm to pass through and should not be climbable by children. Height of the balustrade to be 900mm measured above pitch line. Provide handrail to top of balustrade. Height of balustrade to landings to be 1100mm above finished floor level.

Mezzanine Floor
50 x 150mm timber to be resin bolted to existing brickwork. Second 50 x 150mm bolted to first.
50 x 150mm floor timbers hung from joist hangers at 400mm centres and solid intermediate horizontal noggins at 450mm. With 18mm moisture resistant chipboard flooring to be screwed down.

Internal Walls

50 x 100mm softwood treated timbers studs at 400mm centres with 50 x 100mm head and sole plates and solid intermediate horizontal noggins at 1/3 height or 450mm. Provide min 10kg/m³ density acoustic soundproof quilt (eg. 100mm mineral fibre sound insulation) in all voids the full depth of the stud. Walls faced throughout with 12.5mm plaster board with skim plaster finish. Taped and jointed complete with beads and stops.

Internal Stud Partitions
Partitions built off doubled up joists where partitions run parallel or provide noggins where at right angles, or built off DPC on thickened concrete slab if solid ground floor. Walls faced throughout with 12.5mm plaster board with skim plaster finish. Taped and jointed complete with beads and stops.

Floor
50 x 100mm softwood treated timbers studs at 400mm centres and solid intermediate horizontal noggins at 450mm.. Provide min 10kg/m³ density acoustic soundproof quilt (eg. 100mm mineral fibre sound insulation) in all voids the full depth of the floor. 18mm moisture resistant chipboard flooring to be screwed down.

Drainage
All pipe work to be uPVC and to comply with BS7158 and BS8012005. Soil stacks 110dia with 32dia wastes to wash hand basins, 40dia wastes to shower. Soil pipe to be externally mounted and joined to existing pipework by way of existing manhole.

Rainwater Goods
An uPVC 112mm high capacity storm water system complete with 68mm diameter downpipes. Install rainwater goods in accordance with manufacturers recommendations.

Soffits and Fascia
White uPVC. Soffits with 76mm vents.

If all the drawings, permissions and regulations seem a little bit overwhelming you can of course employ an architect. But before you do, think through the space well and plan a rough idea on paper. That way you are more likely to get what you want and hopefully the bill will be smaller.

Make sure you check with the architect what you are getting for their fee. Will they include structural calculations, submission of plans to the council for planning and building regulations.

I would like to add though that you can have a go, after all you might surprise yourself. If you have been able to do the drawings, checked with the council regarding permissions, applied and then been granted the go ahead, you would have saved yourself quite a chunk of the budget.

Overview & Order

When undertaking building work there is not a set and rigid order for works. Many tasks are dependent on other jobs being part finished or completed.

Below I have given a rough idea in which the tasks should be completed. You will see that there are several overlaps and consecutive jobs that are undertaken at one time. The work described here is detailed in the following pages and can be found on the contents page.

Main Job Description	Other work that can be undertaken from this point	
Idea		
Check foundations		
Plan services		
Draw Plans	Maybe employ architect	
Structural calculations	Employ Structural Engineer	
Apply for planning permission		
Apply for building regulations	Work can commence whilst waiting for building regulations – site visit from building inspector	
Clear existing conversion space		
Removal of unwanted structures (roof, non-structural walls etc)		
External Structures – beams and lintels, roof trusses		Main drainage and sewer pipes can be installed up to the building
Cover roof – flat roof (3 layer felt) or pitched roof (felt, batten and tile)		
Guttering, fascia, downpipes		
Internal damp proofing		
Add windows / door		
Dry line and add internal structures		
Electricity cables installed	Internet and TV cables	

Water feed pipes installed		Pipes for shower room or washroom installed under floor	
Insulate – walls, floor, ceiling			
Flooring – boards or concrete screed			
Plaster board	Cut holes for recessed lights, sockets, switches		
Plaster		Painting – begin with contact emulsion	
Connect electricity			Install heating
Drainage – waste pipes through walls	Link with water feed and waste		
Internal work and storage			
Stairs and balustrade			Wood work installation as rooms begin to get completed
Floor covering for kitchen and wash room area			
Shower room – tile, install sanitary ware			
Toilet - install			
Kitchen installation			
Painting walls and wood work final coat			
Carpet		Touch up paint	
Furnishing			

BEFORE YOU BEGIN

Budget

Building a Tiny House is a lot cheaper than building a house but it still costs. We were able to use our own skills to cut the price. Another way to reduce the bill is to manage the different trades yourself, although this may be more stressful. Budget will need to be set aside for: plans and drawings, structural calculations (and maybe a site visit), skips and waste removal, timber, fixings (screws, bolts, nails, etc ...), tiles, roofing felt, guttering, concrete, electrics, plasterboard, plaster/plasterer, stairs, pipes, windows, sanitary ware, storage ... Quite a bit will be required. Be sensible with your budget. You don't want to overspend because of lack of planning.

Below are some tables that you might find useful with working out your budget.

Planning or Before Works			
Drawings		New garage/shed	
Structural calculations		Site clearance for new	
Planning permission fee			
Building regulations fee		Labour	

Building Works - Exterior			
Site clearance		Windows	
Skips		Doors	
Bricks		Drainage excavation	
Blocks		Drainage pipes	
Beams		Water supply	
Lintels		Electricity supply	
Timber (roof)		Gas supply	
Roofing felt		Sealant	
Battens			
Tiles		Cement	
Fixings (nails, screws)		Concrete	
Guttering		Scaffolding/ladder	
Fascia & Soffits			
Roof windows		Labour	

Building Works - Interior

Site clearance		Water pipes	
Skips		Water wastes	
Damp proof lining (paint)		Plaster board	
Timber – wall/floor lining		Plaster	
Insulation - floor		Paint	
Insulation - walls		Heaters	
Insulation - roof		Water heater	
Timber – partition walls		Extractor fan (shower)	
Timber – structural floors		Stairs and rails	
Flooring (chipboard)		Skirting	
Fixings (nails, screws)		Architrave	
Electrics - cable		Door	
Electrics – fuse box			
Electrics – stitches/power points		Labour	

Fixtures/Furnishings			
Shower tray		Storage solutions	
Toilet		Worktop	
Basin/vanity unit		Carpet	
Taps		Floor covering	
Shower		Curtains	
Shower screen		Blinds	
Tiles		Appliances	
Grout			
Sealant		Other:	
Kitchen cupboards			
Kitchen sink			
Taps			
Lights		Labour	

These are not exhaustible lists. Your build will look different to ours and so you will have different needs. The lists do, however, cover the majority.

When pricing up remember that you will probably have to add delivery charges to the property.

One thing you can do to save a little money is to ask about **trade accounts** with the companies that you are buying from.

You can also **hire equipment** instead of buying – this is only a good solution if you know that you will complete the job in the required time. We hired a scaffold tower when we began work. It was such a useful piece of kit, but when we worked out how long we would need the tower for, the hire costs were far more expensive than buying our own tower. In the end we purchased one which has not only been useful in this building project, but will continue to be useful for other building jobs too (such as the extension!). This can, of course be sold on afterwards.

If you are competent and want to have a go at **doing it yourself**, you can find lots of useful videos online and hopefully this book will inspire you to have a go. Some companies will charge quite a bit for doing something simple. It may take you longer to complete, but if time isn't a pressure, the act of creating something like a Tiny House can be extremely rewarding.

There are some skills that are best left to the professionals. In the UK you need to have the electrics certified with a certificate and the windows installed by a FENSA accredited person. But there are still ways round this one. You can install the electrics, allowing a kind electrician to take a look and connect you before giving you the certificate (please check that your electrician will allow you to do this) and windows can be installed by a person if they have liability insurance. You could try a local window manufacturing firm, they may supply the windows and then have a fitters available. Their costs should not be as high as the larger companies.

Services

I have already touched on this subject in the Planning Permission section.

We needed to decide how to supply the services that would be needed in the tiny house. How would the water would get into the tiny house and how it would waste water would be removed? This is worth thinking about in the planning stage because this can be a quite expensive part of the build and you don't even get to see it as it is all buried underground.

You want to be able to link up to your mains water in a simple and efficient way and get the waste water out and into the drain without too much hassle. Try to find your nearest manhole (that is downhill from the waste coming out of the Tiny House) and then think about how the waste can get there.

What type of heating would be best? Ideally, gas would have been a more economical way of heating the water and the space but in order to do this we would have had to have a second gas meter installed so that "both" properties would have the best supply. This would have been a big expense. Therefore, we opted for electric water heaters, shower and heating system. We knew that electricity was not renown for being the most efficient but there was little choice. Researching into the subject meant that we were much happier about doing this. Companies have moved on quite a bit from storage, convectors and fan heaters. We decided to look into oil filled, wall hung radiators that are heated by electricity. Since the Tiny House was going to be very well insulated, we knew that the heating would only be nominal.

The water heating systems are also much better than they used to be. However, do watch out for added fixtures and fittings with these instant water heaters, they don't always some supplied and since the tap will not be 3m away from the heater you will probably need the extra safety vessels and valves.

Before beginning to build we needed to have an idea of the extra electricity needed to run the heaters and radiators, sockets, lighting, cooking facilities. The power ratings on water heaters and radiators can be high and high rating cables are very thick and difficult to install in small spaces because they do not bend and tuck away neatly. It was important to calculate the rating so that the correct cables to the mains could be planned.

A Tiny House could benefit from renewable power sources. It would be great to think about power in terms of solar and wind.

Foundations

I have mentioned a little bit about this when talking about the structural calculations. This is probably a very important point. Back when our house was built in the 1950's, the building regulations were very different. The foundations were shallow and appropriate for the era .... but now when you build an extension to your house, foundations are often three times as deep and twice as wide have to be dug and filled with concrete.

We checked the foundations of the garage by digging out a small section of soil until we reached the top of the concrete then proceeded to dig round that and deeper until the underside of the concrete was found. This measurement was needed for the structural engineer and his calculations for the beam that we were hoping to add.

In the photo you can see the damp proof course (black line) just above the soil level. There are then four courses of brick. After that there is the top of the concrete foundations. The structural engineer took the measurements to the foundation slab of concrete, the distance it came out from the wall and the depth of the slab.

Thankfully, the foundations were enough for us to use. If they weren't we would have had to either; arranged for deeper foundations to be made or for the new part of the structure to be carried by internal framing thus reducing the already limited internal space.

TEAR DOWN ...

Clearing the way

Our journey to building a Tiny House had to begin with finding a new place to store all the stuff that was currently in our brick garage. Our house is located on a triangular plot and has a very large front garden. It is also in an unusual position in that the front garden isn't next to any road. (When we bought the house we had no idea what size the garden was as it was so overgrown - but that is a different story.) The decision to put a "new" garage in the front garden was made. Because of the positioning of the house and garden, planning permission wasn't required, but we added it to our application to ensure that there would not be any problems later on.

We researched the cost of a new garage and they were expensive taking a large percentage to the budget. We took an alternative route. We turned to ebay and grabbed ourselves a bargain. We picked up a prefabricated concrete garage for just 99p! It would need transporting home, a new roof since the existing was asbestos (the seller even removed this for us at no extra cost) and a concrete base would need to be laid, but it was still very good value.

To lay a concrete base for the new structure an area was cleared and sectioned off using treated timber. The tops of the timber were carefully levelled with each other so that when the concrete arrived and was being laid the slab would be level.

The base was filled to 100mm from the top edge with hardcore. As you can see we had a mixture of hardcore taken from numerous building jobs that my husband had completed. The hardcore was mostly broken bricks fairly neatly arranged so that the concrete would have a strong base. Roof tiles and floor/wall tiles are not idea as there is very little strength in them. You can see a thin layer of tiles in the photo but these lay on top of the broken brick base.

You can often pick up hardcore for free from ads in the paper or online. Generally, builders are happy to give it away because it costs to have it disposed of.

When we considered the cost of the concrete we came to the conclusion that having ready mixed concrete delivered was the most economical. To mix this volume of concrete, using a hired mixer with delivered ballast, sand and cement was roughly the same price, plus it would take a couple of days to do the mixing.

If a mixer arrived with the ready mixed load and a couple of friends with wheelbarrows could be arranged, the task would be complete in a morning.

Using a long timber that stretched from one side to the other, the concrete could be tampered and levelled. The effort in levelling the timber edges at the beginning pays off at this point.

The base needed to prove before the new building was erected.

This type of concrete slab can be used as a base for a timber Tiny House. Please check the regulations for your area regarding depths and levels.

The wall sections were very heavy, but they slotted together easily.

It was not very pretty, but with a coat of paint it could look great.

A couple of the windows were broken but they could easily be repaired. The glass cost more than the garage! In fact, we turned it into a learning opportunity and my husband taught our youngest how to replace the window.

Of course, the stuff that we had accumulated over 20 years of marriage was sorted and the items we were keeping were placed in their new home along with several boxes of boot sale items.

The finished front garden garage sits quite comfortably in the garden now. We are hoping to grow some plants up the walls for a bit of colour and texture. Overall, a successful start to the project.

We could now focus on the garage to Tiny House conversion.

The brick garage is only 3 metres wide and a little under 7 metres long, but we had big plans for it as it appeared to be a good size for conversion with few tweaks here and there. Being detached from the house would create a few issues regarding services but would also be an added bonus for anyone who could use it as a tiny house. As it stood it had a broken and rotten wooden garage door, a sticky side entrance with two small side windows (one of which was broken) and a further window which looked over the back garden. The roof leaked a little and was made of asbestos.

The first thing we needed to do was knock this 1950's garage into shape. The roof was removed and disposed of safely as it contained asbestos. This is something that you should not attempt to do by yourself due to the health risks - get some quotes, budget and get a company to sort it out. It is so much better to be safe than to save a little bit of cash. Companies can be found in the telephone directory, can be recommended by others or, as ever, online. They should be wearing masks and protective gear while working. They will probably double wrap the asbestos to safely take away.

Inside the brick garage there were some internal walls, a coal bunker and redundant roof trusses These were not needed as part of the design so had to go.

A little bit of muscle and enthusiasm go a long way to shifting bricks. Normally, in a structure like a garage, the bricks will be tied into the exterior wall so take care when knocking them out. Use a hammer and baluster between the bricks on the render. You may need to cut the bricks where they are tied into the wall with an angle grinder.

We started from the top of the wall and worked our way down removing a few bricks at a time. Slow and steady, avoiding taking out whole rows in one go. We did not want to demolish what we already had in place. If you are trying this you could consider recycling the bricks. They can be used for hardcore for a concrete base, used by local builders or even advertised as free to collect for someone else's building project.

Next, the slightly sloped side walls would needed to be addressed since we were going to lay a couple of extra courses of bricks to raise the height of the walls. The height would match the soldier course at the front of the garage. The incomplete and cut bricks were removed from the top edge of the walls. At this point, if there were any loose bricks they were also removed.

We were left with a roofless brick shell, that quite frankly, looked like it would be too small to do anything with. But with plans in hand, I was confident that there would be enough space when we had finished with it.

... AND BUILD UP

Structures

The garage was looking in a sorry state and nothing like a Tiny House. It had no roof and even the brick walls were a little sad.

Having spoken to and had a visit from the structural engineer, we were ready to start putting it all back together. The structural calculations told us what beams, lintels and other structural elements needed to be fitted.

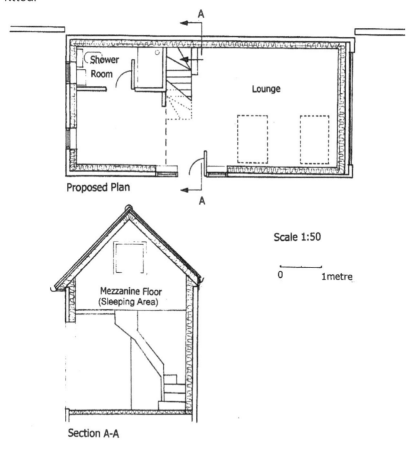

Shower Room

Lounge

Proposed Plan

A

Scale 1:50

0   1metre

Mezzanine Floor
(Sleeping Area)

Section A-A

The new layout would consist of an open plan space to the right as you walked in. This would be the lounge/dining space. To the left would be the kitchen area and the shower room would be accessed through the kitchen. The larger open space would have stairs to the mezzanine floor (above the kitchen and shower room).

Many Tiny Houses use ladders to access higher levels. In traditional Tiny Houses that are on wheels, the bulk of stairs would add weight to the trailer and possibly take up too much space. We decided that even though stairs would use more floor space than a ladder, it would be safer in those dark trips to the toilet in the night, and they feel more permanent within a home setting. Also the space below the stairs could be made use of for storage a possibly a desk or table.

The mezzanine was where the bedroom/sleeping area would be situated. From here you could look out over the lounge. The choice to keep the lounge more open was to create an illusion of space. The vaulted ceiling with roof lights would mean that the room was light.

With a small space it is very easy to make it appear even smaller. If there is a way of making the person in the room feel like they inhabit less room, the space will have the illusion of being bigger. The open, vaulted ceiling will create an optical scale.

The structural elements that needed to be added were:
*The steel beam holding the roof – this would span from one end of the Tiny House to the other.
*The lintel in the new window openings – window in the shower room and in the sleeping area on the mezzanine floor.
*The lintel over the door and windows – the existing lintels were not structurally sound and new loads were to be added to this area so a new lintel was needed.
*The joists to the mezzanine floor – the sleeping area would be supported by the walls and span from one side to the other.

First the walls were built up by a few courses to match the height of the front of the garage. We were able to use recycled bricks from another wall we were removing (we are in the midst of an extension to the main house).

Brick sizes have changed over time with the introduction of metric sizes with the imperial size bricks being discontinued. Depending on when your property was built, you may have either metric or imperial sized bricks. Older style bricks can be sourced with reclamation yards, auction sites and local building projects but they tend to be more expensive as they have been removed with care to retain the whole brick.

It is also important to match the colour and style of brick as much as possible or they will appear obvious to the final project and ruin the overall effect. You can use new bricks but be aware that the sizes may not match. Try to take a couple of sample bricks with you when looking for "new" bricks for your build.

A new window was cut into the wall for the shower room. The cuts were made with an angle grinder and used the existing brick pattern as a guide. The sides of the window followed the ends on every other brick and cut half way through the others. Cutting the window like this will give the appearance that the window was always meant to be there rather than an after-thought. The window size was not widened because of the structural calculations. The new windows to the shower room and the kitchen would be made taller by cutting out the brick work below.

You can see from these photos, the new bricks appear to have a different surface colour, but this is only due to weathering. The older, existing bricks can be pressure cleaned or the new bricks left to weather naturally.

The photo also shows that one of the windows next to the door has been filled with bricks. This was a slight design change from the original plans. Having looked at the loads that the mezzanine floor would exert onto the top of the left hand window by the door, we decided to not have the window at all but extend the external wall. We didn't have to do this. A larger and stronger lintel could have been used above the window but this would have then raised the mezzanine floor and given less head room in the sleeping area. This was a design choice.

The lintels were installed above the window openings before the bricks were laid. The lintel cannot be seen when the doors and window are fitted.

At the end walls we needed to create the triangular section that would give us a pitched roof. These gables were originally planned to be formed out of timber but after the structural engineer visit and discussions about loads to the walls, block work was agreed. The blocks would be able to carry the load of the steel beam, roof and tiles down and into the wall evenly. At this point the new window opening in the gable was designed around the pattern of the blocks. It was quite convenient that the block work structure fitted the triangular gable so well.

Building the walls from the inside rather than from the outside created a slight problem. The outside appearance of the morta r needs to be neat and tidy whereas the inside would be hidden behind the internal walls.

The blocks were laid from a scaffold tower. This equipment can be hired or bought. Buying a scaffold tower for this project was a good decision as it made so many of the jobs easier and safer.

The block work would be clad on the outside by tile hanging. This would match our property. When thinking about the details of the appearance of your build, it is best to either match existing building nearby or be completely different. If you aim for being somewhere between the two you will probably end up will an unsatisfactory looking building.

When both ends were built up, the steel beam was due to be installed. We decided to insert the beam as a whole length instead of in sections and bolting them together. The beam was too heavy for a person to handle so a local firm collected it from the company where we had it made, delivered it to our property and lifted the beam into place via a crane.

The steel beam was guided (thankfully very expertly) past the side of the house and onto the pad-stones that sat on the block work. The photo bottom left also shows the concrete lintel that spans the window.

There was something oddly satisfying in seeing the beam sitting squarely on the padsone. Up to the point where the crane untied the load and let it rest, there was always the question of did we measure the length right.

The photo shows the beam resting in place. You can also see the wall plate in place ready to take the roof timbers. This is timber fixed to the top edge of wall and fixed with mortar and screws.

To actually be putting the tiny house together rather than tearing it down is a much more positive place to be! With the beam resting on the tops of the walls the garage felt strangely different. It was beginning to take shape.

EXTERNAL WORK

Roof Structure

Now that the beam was sitting nicely in place, the roof could begin to take shape. Inserting new roof timbers would give a guide to finish the block work gable ends.

The roof timbers were cut and fixed to the timber ridge plate that sits on top of the beam. The building inspector suggested strapping the rafters to the beam for extra security. This method would ensure that a strong wind would not shift the roof since all the members were joined together.

Cutting the angles can be a little tricky. The top of the rafter needs to fit neatly and snugly against its opposite rafter. The right angle notch at the beam and at the wall plate also need to be taken out allowing for the pitch of the roof. It would have been simple to make one rafter and then just copy it several times, only buildings tend not to be exactly square. A template rafter was used for a few rafters, checking to see if it sat well before cutting the next.

Who said you never use maths in real life? I would want to work these angles out on paper first but my husband is experienced enough to just go with it and work them out on site.

The rafter can be laid against the wall plate and ridge plate (on top of beam) this will give you an accurate angle of the pitch of the roof. A vertical line should be marked at the top of the rafter, keeping the top point of the vertical line at the very end of the timber. You could use a plumb line or a set square measured from the top of the ridge plate and onto the timber.

Now move the rafter so that the lowest point of the vertical line is touching the ridge plate edge/corner. Mark this place with a horizontal line. Making sure that the rafter is reaching down to the wall plate with the timber face at a right angle (not drifting off to one side) mark the place where the timber touches the edge/corner of the wall plate with a horizontal line. These two horizontal lines will become the top edge of the right angle notch that needs to be removed. The depth of the notches will be determined by the structural drawings and the size of the timbers specified.

The rafters were spaced 400mm centres (40cm between the rafters).

The rafters sit on the wall plate. When they are fixed in place the ends of the rafters will overhang the wall too far. Wait until all the rafters are in place before you cut them to length.

Work out how wide the soffit is and measure from the outside wall to the required distance. Mark a vertical line on the rafter and cut. Mark a horizontal line on the rafter giving a right angle to the lower end of the timber. This should be approximately between 150 and 200mm from the bottom of the wall plate. Each rafter should be marked individually for an even edge.

The steel beam allowed for us to have an open roof structure without the truss spanning timbers which would normally stop the roof from splaying. This would provide the headroom above the stairs and in the bedroom area. The main living area would have a high ceiling.

Roof Windows

The original design had two roof windows but we changed this to a single but a slightly larger one. The rafters were carefully thought out so that the window would fit into the roof between two rafters with one cut rafter in between the frame. As the opening had to cut through one rafter, the frame would be double trimmed and strapped to maintain strength.

The double trimmers are basically two pieces of timber fixed together and strapped. The photo shows a later development with the insulation in place, but this allows you to see the rafters better.

We placed the window in this position considering the plastering requirements. In order to get a neat and durable plaster finish we did not want the window too close to the top of the wall. The window was not taller because the plastering of the ridge section would have a slightly curved profile. (See page 70 with ceiling plastered.)

Roof windows should be fitted to the manufacturers specifications. You will probably need to purchase a window and the flashing kit with it. It is also advisable to leave fitting the window until you are committed to tile since the window fits into and onto the tiled area.

The felt was cut away at the site where the window was to be fitted and any loose felt was fixed in place.

The window was removed from the frame using release clips. The frame could then be used to mark the cutting points on the rafter that ran through the centre of the site. An allowance was made as per instructions supplied with the window. At this point the double trimmer timbers were added and fixed into position. The window frame was then fixed into place using the fixtures supplied.

The rest of the window could not be installed until the tiling had been completed up to the bottom of the window.

When the tiles were in line with the lower edge the flashings were fitted into place. Again the flashing should be fitted following the specific instructions with the window.

The tiles were cut so that they sat up against the tile stops on the flashing at either side or fixed into place using eaves and standard tiles at the top. The double glazed unit was then put back into the frame.

Roof Tiles

Roof tiles can be all sorts of colours, materials and profiles.

We tried to match the roof tiles of the Tiny House to the main house. Tiles can be found in free to collect adverts and we found half of the tiles we needed from such an advert from a local property. They were fitted on one side of the roof of the Tiny House, whilst on the other, new tiles were used. Since you cannot view both sides at the same time, the only thing that would give it away is the ridge on the wrong side. Tiles are an expensive outlay to a project so if you can recycle some you may find that a good saving can be made.

The gaps between the roof and the wall were filled with cut blocks. The roof line helped to provide a pattern for cutting the black to size.

Breathable felt was run from one gable end to the other starting on at the eaves as the lowest layer. Further layers overlapped a little adding extra protection against moisture.

At the gable ends, cement boards were secured under the felt edge by nailing down onto the rafters allowing for sufficient overhang for gable end to be felt, battened and tile hung. The cement boards do not need to too wide, 300mm was wide enough for our purposes. The tile battens are then added, cutting them about 20mm short from the edge of the roof. The batten for the first row of tiles was then offered up to the roof. An eaves tile was hooked onto the top edge. The batten was then fixed through the felt to the timber trusses. The next batten position is dictated by the full roof tile's length. We offered up the batten with a standard roof tile hooked to the top. When the bottom edges were lined up neatly the batten was fixed into place. The spacing of the battens from now on should be even as the tiles should overlap each other at the same distance apart.

Tiles can be fixed with two nails but this is not necessary. Every fifth row should be secured. Some tiles also needed to be cut using the angle grinder. You may also need some "tile and a half" tiles to complete the rows as tiles cannot be fixed in place if too small.

The top row of tiles, were again the shorter eaves tiles. These were then capped with the ridge tiles fixed into place with mortar. The edge between the tile and the concrete board was also finished off with mortar.

Detail of the gable showing some different tile types. Ridge (curved top tile) eaves (shorter tile) standard tile and reclaimed tiles used for hanging on the gable ends. The concrete board can also be seen and the edges have been filled with mortar. Before mortar is added, small scrunched up bits of newspaper can be pushed into the gaps to stop the pug from being pushed in too far.

Tile Hanging

Tile hanging the gable ends was part of the design since it tied in with the design of our property. Again, in order for the new Tiny House to feel like it hasn't just landed out of thin air, the exterior design was considered carefully.

The method for tile hanging is similar to the fitting the tiles to the roof. We used reclaimed tiles that matched out property and were picked up for free using an online community where instead of going to landfill, your unwanted items are advertised and free for others.

It is not necessary to add felt under the battens, but for extra protection we added a layer of the breathable felt we had used on the roof.

The first batten row, at the very bottom of the area to be tile hung, is doubled to allow for the tiles to sit at the correct angle away from the wall.

This photo shows the street facing end of the Tiny House. It is a simple flat area. However, the garden facing gable had a window in the design.

Photo shows double batten at bottom, eaves tile, staggered tiling and render to the roof tiles making a neat end.

The same spacing applied to the battens at the rear of the Tiny House, only on this face there was a gap for the window.

The tiles were hung in a staggered arrangement from the battens and fixed in place with nails. Tiles were carefully cut with an angle grinder at the gable edges to fit.

Tiles could be fitted up to the window opening but then lead flashing needed to be applied to ensure a watertight fitting for the window against the tiles. Lead was used as it is a very pliable metal. It may look like a simple job to apply but it is actually skilled. We wanted to be confident that a watertight seal would be made, so arranged for a skilled friend to do the lead work. A small opening like this was completed very quickly.

There are many videos available online that could guide you. However, if you are not confident that you have the patience to learn and finance to make mistakes, sometimes it is better to employ someone else.

The window was fitted after the lead was in place.

Some building projects may require a brick face or rendered surface instead of a tile hung face. A brick faced wall will be more expensive in materials and labour because of the time it takes to lay the bricks. A rendered wall can be made over a mesh/chicken wire covered timber wall or a block wall. Rendering is a difficult skill to master, so if you are planning on doing only a small section you may be able to get away with it, but on larger surfaces, it would probably same you time and money to have a skilled person give the wall a good rendered surface. You may find that same person is able to help with the internal plastering too.

Windows and Door

The old wooden single glazed windows were replaced with double glazed units. The kitchen window was lengthened and the shower room window cut out of the brickwork using an angle grinder. A new double glazed door was fitted with a side window.

If you are looking to sell you will require a Fensa recognised fitter or an insured builder/yourself to install windows and doors.

Before we measured and fitted the door we needed to raise the threshold as the new insulated floor would raise the existing floor level by 100mm for the insulation plus the depth of the flooring on top of that. We added a course of bricks along the bottom of the door opening to raise the threshold.

There are two steps up that lead to the door and adding the course of bricks, along with the door frame, made the "third step" into the Tiny House an even rise. It is generally better to give steps equal heights for safety and convenience.

Since we do not have many windows in the main open area of the Tiny House, we chose to have a single glass door rather than a solid panel to keep light streaming into the internal space.

The windows sizes where determined by the design of the interior and the aesthetic appearance of the brick wall. We did not want to cut a window opening randomly into the brick face but used the pug lines of the brick courses to help design the windows.

Windows can be bought ready made in certain sizes from DIY and builders' merchants and some money can be saved by doing this. Do remember that for fire safety at least one window in each space must be big enough to climb through and have hinges that allow the window to open fully.

Also, don't forget to think about what glass you need. We had obscure glass for the shower room and toughened safety glass for the door.

New windows and door ensure a draught free and secure space.

Guttering

We wanted to use the void inside the soffits to introduce and hide the electricity and water into the tiny house. This was the best option and allow us to not disrupt the internal space too much.

After the rafter ends were cut to length, they were then boxed in with thin ply running the length of the building on both the cut edges. The ply was fixed so that it went up under the tiles and overhanging felt and also back to the brick wall.

The photos show the cut ends of the roof trusses and then the boxing in of the trusses with treated ply. The second photo also shows the thick electricity supply cable that came from our property and into the Tiny House. The water supply was also fed into the house at the same point.

The uPVC soffits and fascia were cut and fixed into place. This is much easier with two people. The soffit is fixed to the underside first with the fascia catching the front edge when it is screwed into place. The screws are covered by screw caps. The exposed ends are finished neatly with further plastic. Where the soffit meets the wall a bead of silicone should be applied to fill any gaps.

By using uPVC it gives an almost maintenance free solution. The plastic should be cleaned occasionally.

The guttering was installed allowing for a slight fall so that the water coming off the roof would drain away into the downpipe. The first gutter bracket was fixed at the far end and string tied to the bracket. The string was then stretched to the position of the downpipe. A spirit level determined if there was enough downward angle between the first bracket and the downpipe before other brackets were fitted. The guttering was then snapped into place and tested to check the flow with a little water. All the guttering runs downhill into the downpipe be it the long length or short length.

The existing garage had guttering and a drain to carry away the rain water. We used this existing drain on the one side of the garage. On the other side of the garage there was no drain as the slant of the roof carried all the rain water to the one side.

The new guttering on the far side was fed into a soak away, much like the new garage we had added to our front garden. A cubic meter hole should be dug and three quarters of that needs to be filled with clean hardcore. The rainwater should be fed into the hole using a drainpipe. A concrete slab should be placed over the top resting on a rim so that it doesn't collapse into the soakaway. You can purchase a soakwell which will also do the same job. Soakwells are usually made of plastic or fibreglass and are buried in the ground in a similar way.

Drainage

This is another of the jobs that can take a fair amount of time yet appears that you have done very little, it is however, essential. You cannot begin this job until you know where the toilet, basin, shower and kitchen sink will be located. You may even need to work on this task on and off until fairly near completion of the build because of the need to fit the toilet, basin, shower and kitchen sink.

Below are a series of photos showing the installation of the soil pipe.

1

2

3

4

5

6

7

8

9   10   11

Photo 1: 110mm waste pipe leaves the Tiny House (lined up with the waste hole in the back of the toilet). Rodding access needed at this point because of the configiration of bends in the waste pipe.

Photo 2: Another right angle directs the waste along the outside wall.

Photo 3: An awkward bend can be overcome by an adjustable angle fitting.

Photo 4: Surface mounted waste pipe with a fall to allow for waste tot be washed away. The pipe can be run underground but in our case , with the differing levels of the garden, surface mounting was the best option.

Photo 5: Paving slab that was adjacent to the manhole was cut with an angle grinder. The hole was then dug for the pipe to sit at a slight fall towards the drain.

Photo 6: Hole drilled into the side wall of the drain for the pipe to be inserted.

Photo 7: Pipe is inserted trough the drain wall and angled so that the waste is able to flow away.

Photo 8: Pipe runs from the Tiny House down to the drain – all the connections have been made and tested.

Photo 9: Access to the pipe for rodding in case of blockage is above ground.

Photo 10: Pipe surrounded by pea shingle underground so that there is warning of the pipe being there.

Photo 11: Cut paving slabs put back and cemented into place.

Below are some more images showing the connection between the drainage pipes to the installed waste pipe.

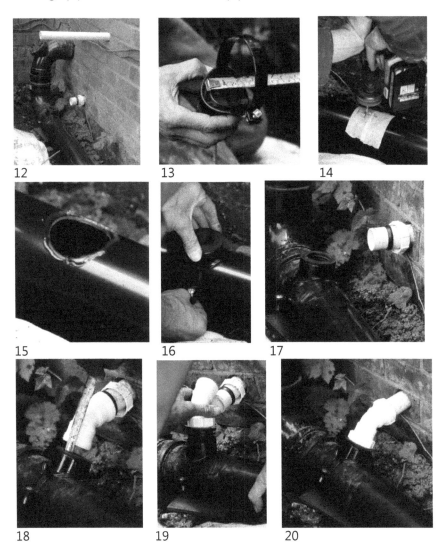

12

13

14

15

16

17

18

19

20

21 22 23

24

Photo 12: Drainage pipes are fitted through wall by drilling.
Photo 13: Internal diameter of boss connector measured.
Photo 14: Masking tape applied to waste pipe and centre marked directly below drainage pipe. Hole drilled to the same diameter.
Photo 15: Line of sealant applied to waste pipe.
Photo 16: Boss connector fitted in place and tightened.
Photo 17: Screw fixing for elbow inserted onto drainage pipe.
Photo 18: Distance between drainage pipe elbow and waste pipe measured. Take into account the amount of pipe needed to be inserted inside fittings.
Photo 19: Fit the new pipe. May require a bit of twisting and shoving for tight fit.
Photo 20: Shower drainage pipe complete.
Photo 21: Mark positon (as before) for other drainage. Use a spirit level.
Photo 22: Fit elbows as before and measure length of pipe needed.
Photo 23: Fit new down pipe.
Photo 24: Seal the around the drainage and waste pipe wall exits.

INTERNAL WORK

Electric

The cable supplying electricity from the main property to the Tiny House is thick. It is needed for the heating, water heater, shower, cooker, lighting and power sockets.

Electricity is not a DIY job. If you feel confident and are competent you can lay the cables and circuits, but check with your electrician first. Some electricians are happy to connect you up and give you a certificate if they can see what you have done but others may not.

When considering what electricity we needed in the Tiny House, we visualised what we use every day and then thought about how to incorporate these things into the Tiny House without using too much space. The loads were then calculated and the correct cables used.

The electricity wasn't installed in one go as walls and ceilings needed to be created beforehand.

The consumer unit would be sited up high where the switches could still be accessed from the mezzanine, but out of the way from the main living area. From here all the other cables would be run. We needed to find a solution to get the cable to this position.

Planning was the key. Before the walls could be finished all the sockets and switches had to be finalised.

We chose to have a four way light switch by the front door. This switch would operate the lights in the kitchen, lounge, bedroom and outside. A further switch to operate the bedroom would be required on the mezzanine. The shower room would have a pull cord inside room, but would also require a switch for the shower and ventilation fan. These would be situated outside the room.

The lounge, bedroom and shower room would be heated with wall hung, oil filled radiators which would have timers. The cable for these had to be installed before the walls too.

Lighting in the Tiny House was also thought about. In the area where the ceiling would be low, inset spots would be fitted. This included the bedroom, kitchen and shower room. The shower room needed to have a waterproof version.

The lounge would have a very high ceiling. If there was pendant lighting in this space it would be difficult to change the bulbs. We opted for wall lights to light the space, knowing that there would be ample surfaces to bounce the light off.

Sockets were decided on and their positions noted. We needed to think about the layouts and use of the rooms in order to decide on how many sockets.

The cables needed to be laid in the right places, however, not all the ceilings/floors were in built so this was an ongoing part of the conversion.

Being a small space it was important not to clutter up the walls and surfaces with switches and sockets.

When positioning cables you can drill through the wood timbers but remember to keep the cables deep enough not to be affected by the fixings you may use on the floor or walls. The drilled hole should be big enough to thread the hole but not too big or the cable may get snagged.

Water

The water and electricity had to come from the main house to the Tiny House. As the two buildings were not connected we needed to bridge the gap.

To dig up the concrete path, lay the cable and water pipe then introduce through the wall and internal floor and make good was a high cost. Instead we created an external connection high up and concealed the cable and pipe in the eaves. It wasn't particularly pretty but would meet the need without too much interference. The cable and water could then be fed into the Tiny House at a convenient place without disturbing the internal space and causing issues with walls or floors. The cable and water pipe were completely insulated to stop damage and cold getting in.

By introducing the water at this high point the pipes could be mostly hidden in the wall and mezzanine floor cavity. They could also be accessed easily without disturbing the existing structure or floor.

The bridge may not be attractive to look at but as it is higher than eye level it is not noticed. The insulation will be covered and enclosed in plastic.

Walls

The walls of the garage were single skinned and would not hold heat very well. Building regulations change over time but no matter what, insulating walls has to be done. The amount of money spent on insulation can be reaped in rewards of a cosy space in the winter and a cool space in the summer, not really mentioning the money saved on bills.

Before we could begin dry lining the walls with a timber frame and insulating, the interior needed to be coated with black moisture barrier paint. At first, we thought 1m high would be enough, but we needed to coat the entire brick surface instead. The garage had a damp proof course but as it would be a single skin structure, the building officer asked for all the entire walls to be treated to eliminate the risk of damp. It really isn't worth leaving this even though it is a boring and rather unrewarding task. We gave the walls the two recommended coats.

In order for the walls to have a good U-value, they needed to be insulated and a timber frame installed for structure.

The wall timbers were fixed at the base to a freestanding timber frame that went around the whole of the floor. They were fixed to the roof trusses at the top. If they had been fixed to the brick work, the holes that were made would have needed to be sealed with silicone or barrier paint.

Cables and insulation would then be inserted into the walls before plaster boarding the surface. When fixing the timber to the walls the spacing of the upright timbers and noggins (the smaller horizontal timbers) were determined by the plasterboard size. We wanted to ensure that fixing the plasterboard would be simple later.

Thermal insulation boards come in multiple thicknesses and sheet sizes. We required 90mm thickness for the walls and floor. The sheets can be cut to size with a saw (although this does blunt the blade so using an old saw is a good idea). The cut sections can then be pushed into the gaps until flush with the timbers. A small gap between the brickwork and the back side of the insulation is recommended. The shiny surface should be interior facing. It seems a shame to be spending such a lot of the budget on something that is never seen, but remember, this will save you money in heating the building later.

Before the insulation is inserted, electric cables and pipes need to be put into place if they are running down the walls. Use your plans to decide where the sockets, light switches, heaters, cooker etc.... will be. It needs to be relatively accurate but there is room for a little movement within the timber frame.

Special attention needs to be paid to the corners where the timber frame could prevent insulation being inserted. If theses spaces are left without insulation, cold spots can be formed and condensation and ultimately damp become a problem.

It was a relief to hide the dark walls behind the insulation and begin to see the potential of the space with some light in it.

Floor

The existing floor in the garage was a concrete slab. In order to fulfil building regulations the new floor would need to be insulated.

This extra height would affect the door and it would not open unless we also raised the threshold with an extra course of bricks. (See Windows and Door section for photo and explanation.)

Since the structure of the concrete slab was not certain and there was probably no moisture barrier in the floor when it was built, we needed to protect the interior from damp. We applied two coats of the moisture resistant paint to this surface too. The Tiny House looked dark and lifeless!

A timber frame was laid paying particular attention to the size of the chipboard floor that needed to be fixed to it ultimately. The noggins between the joists allowed for the flooring to be screwed securely and added extra strength with the joints of the chipboard flooring meeting at the joists. The joists were not screwed into the floor as this would have broken the water barrier we had created, but were instead fixed to each other and the timber frame that supported the walls. In essence, all the timbers were fixed to one another.

The photos show the black walls, raised door threshold, timber joist frame, insulation and chipboard.

We used solid insulation as this allowed for a thinner floor and therefore, more head height. The fibreglass loft insulation could be used but more space has to be given for the insulation to trap the air and work properly.

A useful tip at this point is to mark on the floor where you have the joists and wall timbers. This will make fixing things to the walls at a later point much easier as you will know where there is something solid to screw into. It will also warn you of potential hazards such as cables and pipes. Mark close enough to the wall and be bold, you do not want to lose the markers under the plasterboard, plastering or skirting.

Ceiling

Insulating the ceiling or roof is done in much the same way as the walls and floor. We took care in ensuring that there were not any cold spots where insulation was not fitted. The insulation needed to be 140mm thick between the rafters giving about 10mm between the back of the insulation sheets and the underside of the felt. Then another layer of insulation 15mm was overlaid across the entire roof. This was screwed to the roof rafters.

As there was no room above the beam there is no need for fire board to be fitted around the beam.

Mezzanine

The mezzanine floor was an important structural element in the Tiny House. It would create further living space and a different viewpoint.

First, 150mm x 50mm timber was bolted to the wall two opposite walls using shield anchor bolts.

The joists were then hung from this timber so that they spanned the width of the space from wall to wall. These joists were spaced at 400mm centres. The first joist was double trimmed (double thickness coach bolted together) to allow for the weight of the stairs. The joists then had noggins fitted into the gaps to stop the timbers twisting and moving.

On top of the mezzanine 22mm chipboard was applied to provide a safe floor surface. The chipboard was staggered.

The electric cables and water pipes were carried inside the mezzanine floor to the correct positions for the two rooms below and the one room above.

Plaster

If you had placed the timber frame inside based on the size of a plasterboard sheet, this next part of the build should be relatively easy if not cumbersome.

We had over 30 sheets of plasterboard delivered to the property. At this point it is worth remembering that many companies will deliver goods at a reasonable price or free of charge depending on what you have ordered and if you have set up an account with them.

The plaster board sheets were fixed to the timber frame with screws and holes for cables or lights cut out before fixing into place. It is at this point that the space starts to be transformed. This is an easier task with two people working together as one can hold whilst the other secures.

The scaffolding tower that we had bought was incredibly useful in reaching the high roof space.

Again, since there was so much plastering to be done we called an experienced plasterer to come and skim coat the newly plaster boarded walls and ceiling. There are many tradespeople that can be found on the web or phone book. There are even groups or directories on the internet that allow you to feedback how good a certain tradesperson is along with their standard and cost of work. However, a highly recommended tradesperson is like gold even if they are not associated with one of those directories, since there workload is through recommendations they do not need to register with those directories.

 Within a couple of days the whole space was transformed and began to look more like a liveable place.

The top photo on the next page shows the view from the lounge area to the kitchen, shower room wall and mezzanine floor. Sockets have been cut into the walls and holes for spot lights made even though a pendant light was being used in the meantime. You can see that the plastering was done in stages and over a few days. In some places the plaster board had not been fitted, even the bedroom window was missing at this point too. The schedule for completing the task is fluid as different jobs are dependent on others being finished. Often, many lose ends will be finalised at about the same time.

The second photo shows the lounge from below the mezzanine. The dark plaster is beginning to lighten as it dries. The apex of the high ceiling was plastered so that it had a slight curve from the beam to the slanted sides. This was so that any irregularities with levels would not be obvious.

Again the scaffold tower was a very useful piece of equipment.

Stairs or Ladder

The issue you are constantly facing in creating a Tiny House is space. There are many ways to make the most of the space that you have. One way might have been to use a ladder instead of stairs.

Our decision to have stairs to access the mezzanine floor was based on several ideals. We wanted the Tiny House to have a homely and permanent feel but also have safety when sleepy visits to the kitchen or shower room were needed. Stairs are fixed in place, are a common feature in a house, do not require too much thought to climb or navigate and add structure to a building. When thinking about the stairs, I had designed a fully integrated storage system as part of the structure involving cupboard and drawer space. This would have been acceptable in that it used and filled the neglected space that a standard stair case would take up. However, we chose a traditional staircase.

The space underneath the stairs would be used as a desk and computer area with files, printers and the like housed under the lower treads. The open space under the flight would hopefully give the sense of permanence and familiarity but also an illusion that the Tiny House was bigger than expected by being able to house a stair case.

The layout for the stairs involved two quarter turns and could not be bought off the shelf. The first step would be next to the far lounge wall and the last step the middle of the mezzanine floor where head height was at its highest. A local carpenter/joiner came to measure the where the stairs would go. At this point the plans had to change a little. In order for the stairs to be supported, a newel post had to be placed in an inconvenient place, but thankfully, not obstruct the door. It was an oversight in my design but I was unable to do anything about it. The only way around not having the post would have been to suspend the stair case from the steel beam above, but even that would have altered where the first stair would be placed and invaded the lounge space.

There was no other alternative (except a ladder which we did not want). The design was finalised .There would be two stairs in the initial straight flight before the first quarter turn. There would also be slightly deeper treads. This would mean that the stairs would be pushed closer to the front door than the drawing originally showed. It was a compromise.

The stair case was measured, ordered and delivered by a local joinery company... in several pieces! They had been put together in the workshop and numbered so we knew that when assembled correctly we would have a staircase. If you are after a straight flight of stairs, these can be ordered online (even ebay and amazon sell them!)

It took a while, but with a little patience and a bit of lateral thinking we were able to construct the staircase

With the alterations, the post would be located at this point.
The door into the Tiny House was changed right at the beginning of the build to open hinged from the left as this was now a complete wall and the window was no longer there due to the support for the mezzanine floor.

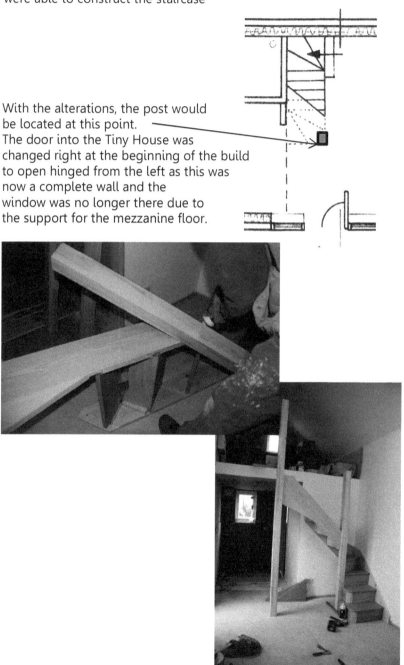

Top left: Showing the twist of the stairs and the open space below.
Top right: The underside of the stairs while uncovered
Bottom: View down the stairs from the mezzanine

Creating a lovely curve below the stairs would be something that we had to tackle a little later in the project when the desk space had been created. The images of the construction of the curve are found here ... but you get to have a sneaky view of the desk and kitchen too!

The plasterer applied wire mesh to create a close fitting curve that hugged the underside of the stairs. Plasterboard was fixed to the flatter area. A bonding coat of plaster was first applied and then a top coat of finished plaster. When dry, this may take a long time because of the thicker layers of plaster, a contact coat and top coat of emulsion can be applied.

The finished curve was well worth the effort and time.

We waited until all the major disruptive work was finished before finishing off the stairs.

There are many ways to balustrade the stairs. Traditional wooden spindles and handrail, or metal versions of the same, cables, rope or glass.

The tiny house needed to have the appearance of space so we chose to install glass.

Firstly we attached the outer side of the steel glass clamps to the outer edges of the posts. The stairs were narrow enough without having the balustrade squeezing the width further.

Next we made up the patterns for the glass out of hardboard. This required a little extra thinking as to what shape we wanted. We echoed the lower wooden sides of the stairs and planned not to have a handrail at all since the glass would suffice.

When we ordered the glass we had to make a sight change since the sharp angle of the internal corner at the bottom of the main piece would create stress. This was changed to form a curve. The glass was 10mm thick toughened safety glass.

The glass was very heavy but was fitted using the glass clamps to hold in place.

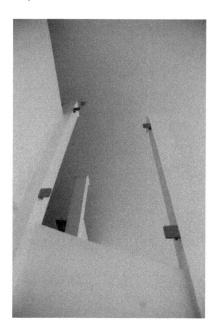

Woodwork

The main woodwork tasks that needed to be completed were the fitting of skirting boards in all the rooms and the door into the shower room.

The wood elements inside the Tiny House were mostly pine. Since this would deepen in colour to a yellow or even orange, we chose to paint it in the main living areas. We oiled the pine shelves in the bedroom area since this was a cosier space and we wanted it to feel less sterile. The warmth of wood in a house is lovely but too much can ruin a space and draw the eye.

The woodwork was undercoated before two coats of white gloss were applied.

Floor Covering

We wanted to keep the floor covering simple. The main living space, bedroom and stairs would be carpeted and the kitchen and shower room would need suitable flooring.

Since the spaces occupied by the kitchen and shower room were next to each other, and to give a sense of flow from the spaces, the flooring would be the same in each.

Originally we were considering tiling the floor with ceramic tiles. This would mean layering the floor with a suitable underlay and then the adhesive and tiles on top. This could alter the amount of head room.

In the end we opted to have vinyl fitted. Our fitter was able to fit the covering in one piece which eliminated any need for thresholds to prevent tripping. The vinyl is also warmer to walk on and things may be less likely to break if dropped onto it.

In the lounge, stairs and bedroom we had carpet fitted. The fitter had previously measured the space and stairs to ensure the correct size was ordered. Fitting carpets is hard on knees but can be done by yourself. Ultimately, it is probably better to get a carpet fitter to do the job for you since they have all the correct tools and will be much quicker.

One way to save money on this part of the job is to purchase the gripper rods and underlay online as this is often the thing that the big carpet companies will charge quite a bit for.

At the doorway coconut matting was laid. In order to prolong the use of the carpet we wanted to create a dirt catching area. This matting is very effective and also allowed for there to be no tripping hazards in or near the kitchen.

The carpet is cut in such a way that the "waste" sections from a larger room can used for the stair treads.

Having the carpet laid is one of the final jobs and really finishes off the space. However, the vinyl needed to be laid before the kitchen was fitted but after the shower tray.

Shower Room

The shower room was determined by the size of the shower tray. We decided to install a large tray as there is nothing worse than having to squeeze into a small shower and then not be able to move.

The external walls were insulated with the solid insulation boards but the internal walls were insulated with 100mm cavity batts that would not only insulate for heat but also for sound.

The walls were then plaster boarded and a skim coat of plaster given. The shower area could have been tiled without the skim coat, but tiling onto a flat surface made it easier.

There is often a lack of space to put shampoo and soap in a shower. We cut a shelf into the wall for this purpose.

Creating drainage from shower tray was quite tricky as it needed to be fitted and tested before the chipboard and floor covering was laid. A slight fall was required on the waste pipe. This meant that the floor joists had to be notched out for the pipe to sit below the chipboard. The shower tray became the template for the correct position for the trap.

We installed an electric shower as this would mean that the water heater that would be in the kitchen could be a smaller and less powerful model. The electric shower would only need a cold water feed and electricity supply. Manufacturer's instructions were followed.

The whole room was not tiled. Only the shower area and beside the vanity unit needed to be protected from water. The shower tray was fitted in place and sealed before the tiles were fitted up to it. The area was sealed again with silicone at all the corners and around the tray. This provided a water tight seal.

The shower enclosure was fitted using the manufacturer's instructions. The walls were painted in a mould resistant paint.

The extractor fan was installed to remove some of the steam generated by the shower, but a window would also be useful in ventilation of the space. This will need an electricity supply and a pull cord switch.

All electrical appliances must have individual isolation switches outside the shower room.

The toilet and vanity unit were fitted in place. The waste pipes had alreay been drilled through the wall before the plastering had been done. It was essential to have the sanitary ware on site early for the purpose of marking out waste and water feeds. When drilling the holes, make sure you have allowed for the finished floor height.

Don't forget the details. A door stop is needed or the door could crash into the shower screen, and a hook for your dressing gown.

The completed shower room feels spacious.

Kitchen

The original kitchen design had to be changed because of the staircase post, but essentially it would be reversed.

The sink and fridge freezer position could not be changed to a more preferable place. The cooker would have to be on the opposite wall but thankfully this all happened before the plastering was done so the electric cables could be rearranged.

When we made up the flat pack carcasses, we moved them about to find the best positioning since the passage space was limited.

The full depth sink unit would contain the water heater unit that would supply hot water to the kitchen sink and hand basin in the shower room.

The narrow floor cupboards to the left of the kitchen galley needed to have a little of the depth taken from the back to allow for more space in the passage way. The photo above shows them with their backs cut and no feet to raise them from the ground. Before we cut the backs we made sure that the drawers would still fit into the cupboard. It was the depth of the drawers that determined how much could be cut off.

The shallow cupboards along the wall would mean that you could wash up in the sink with the drainer in the corner. The worktop on these shallow cupboards would also give a space for food preparation and smaller appliances.

A shallow cupboard was used at the end of the kitchen on the right hand side so that not too much desk space would not be lost.

The wall space on the left hand side of the kitchen was completed using narrow glass fronted cupboards over the sink and then a long open shelving unit. These units that would give a sense of space to this area.

The cupboards were secured to the wall using plasterboard fixings or to the timbers where possible.

Fixing the worktop in place is a relatively easy job but if you have any joints at corners it might be worth getting a carpenter in to give you a neat and water tight corner.

The kitchen area was small but was very functional.

Storage

The Tiny House needed varying types of storage and these would be tackled in different ways.

We would build our own shelving on the mezzanine floor, use flat pack cupboards in the kitchen and lounge and create a desk area under the stairs.

The mezzanine needed to have a rail for safety reasons, but instead of just creating a normal balustrade with spindles we used the space to create a narrow bookshelf. This would also work to divide the space a little and help create a more private and secluded room.

We used the newel posts and the sloped ceiling to mark the end of the shelves.

The book shelf was built in-situ. The lowest shelf was determined by the height of the skirting as it would rest on it at one end and create a continuous level or line around the room.

The height spacers were cut and fixed to the wall and the newel post before the second shelf was cut and fixed. Again spacers were added and the final shelf added. The back edge of the shelf was almost as deep as the newel post. We had allowed for the thickness of some pine cladding to be added to the back of the bookshelf and this would be flush with the edge of the mezzanine. The cladding acted at a stop the shelves so that nothing would fall out the back and a miniature wall to the bedroom space.

The same was repeated to the other side of the staircase and then finishing details such as the trim for the raw edge of the cladding at the top and the joint with the mezzanine were added.

The wood work overlooking the main space was then undercoated and painted white so that it did not stand out too much, as pine has a tendency to darken and yellow with time. The skirting on the mezzanine was also painted but the pine shelves were oiled.

We also wanted there to be some deeper shelves down one side of the room. There was not enough space for a wardrobe (this would be housed in the lounge area) but deeper shelves would mean that folded clothes and other personal items could be close at hand in the bedroom.

The shelf making same method was used as before although the deeper shelves did need extra support in the middle and had to be arranged around the consumer unit that would require access at all times.

The storage for the kitchen and lounge areas was made from flat pack cupboards.

When measuring for a space be sure to remember:

1. Where cupboards meet in a corner, a little extra space is required so that drawers and doors can be opened.

2. Some makes of flat pack furniture will not have a void behind the cupboard for things like pipes and other services.

3. Depths of cupboards can vary with different suppliers.

4. Kitchen cupboards don't have to be used just for kitchens

We had created a double height lounge room but also wanted some great storage. We ordered, constructed and fitted kitchen cupboards to the lounge but used the height to our advantage.

A wide batten was fixed to the wall. The bases of the units would ultimately rest on this timber. It was secured in place through the plaster and into the timber frame using the markings placed on the floor previously. This timber was levelled using a spirit level. By using this method, we knew that all the cupboards would have support that was strong and that they would all be level at the back. Cupboard feet were used to the front edge of the cupboards which allowed for alterations at the front.

We used tall deep cupboards at either side of the space. These would be used as wardrobes, one with two hanging rails for shorter clothing and the other with one. These "kitchen" cupboards were described as cleaning cupboards and had one shelf and one pull out basket. They were ideal for use as wardrobes and were less expensive than the wardrobe units available at the same manufacturer. Also, these cupboards were neutral enough to be used in a living space.

Shallow cupboards were installed in the centre. The two tall units on either side were fixed with shelves. They were fixed to the wall with plasterboard fixings unless the wood frame was conveniently in the right place. In order to find the wood frame underneath the plasterboard, lines were drawn up the wall from the markers made previously on the floor. No lines were drawn in the centre section as this part of the wall would be seen.

The centre of the unit would become a small space for display. The drawers would have worktop fitted and then shelves would be fixed in the gap.

Using different cupboard depths enabled the lounge not to feel cramped.

Other cupboards were secured to the top and bridged the gap in the middle. These storage spaces would be too high to access for everyday items but would act like a small loft. They could be used for seasonal change or occasional use items and would not clutter the all essential space that the Tiny House had.

For the desk area under the stairs, a kitchen wall cupboard was trimmed so that it could fit under the lower turn. It was fitted allowing for the door to open over the carpet.

The same worktop that was used in the kitchen was fixed at the height of a table to make the desk/table surface. The Kitchen worktop was cut at an angle to give as much work surface in the kitchen without taking the desk space away.

Lighting

Lighting is often a thing that gives a room its ambiance so should not be underestimated. You need to be practical and functional but also consider design.

In the areas under the mezzanine we had very little space for pendant lighting. The best solution was to stay simple and have recessed spots in these areas. Since there would also be steam we had to ensure that the fittings were designed for job.

Upstairs in the bedroom, due to the head room, we also opted for recessed spots. These were fitted to one side of the steel beam. Sockets were also available for softer lighting from a lamp.

The lounge offered a different set of problems. With the amazing high ceiling a pendant light fitting would have looked great, but practically would have been difficult to maintain. It would be awkward and possibly dangerous to clean and change the bulbs when the room was full of furniture. However, the large white surface could be used.

We decided to use the ceiling to bounce light back into the room with simple uplighters. By adjusting the angle of the lights a favourable light could be produced.

There were also a few sockets for a work light at the desk and other lamps in the room. I am quite keen on using fairy lights to make a room feel friendly.

Window Dressing

The Tiny House required one last task before it could be moved into. The windows and doors needed to be dressed appropriately for privacy.

We wanted to ensure that the windows were not overly fancy as this would draw the eye. We opted for blinds wherever possible.

The bedroom had blackout fabric applied to the lining so that sleeping would not be too disturbed by morning light.

The roof window could have had a blind fitted and this would have been operated by a pole. We chose to leave the window empty of dressing. I love to watch the clouds and this window acts as a frame to the view of the sky.

The kitchen and shower room both had small roller blinds which would be easy to maintain and hopefully wouldn't retain odours.

Lots of light comes in through the glass door and side window. During the day this is a wonderful feature, but at night and when times of privacy are needed it can cause a problem. There is not enough space above the door for a blind and this method would not be convenient for opening the door. This needed a different method of dressing. We opted for a curtain that could be pushed right back towards the kitchen counter top that would cover the door when closed. A shorter curtain covered the side window.

Tiny House Complete

The following photographs were taken with a fisheye lens. This lens allows you to see the space more fully, although because of the wider angle the image can appear curved.

The Tiny House looks different at night.

The Tiny House is ready to be lived in.

I hope this book has helped you practically. Please let me know if you have enjoyed our journey and if it has inspired you too.
info@katyhollway.com